EARTH ONE

Written by **J. Michael Straczynski**

Pencils by **Shane Davis**

Inks by Sandra Hope

Colors by Barbara Ciardo

Lettered by Rob Leigh

Superman created by Jerry Siegel and Joe Shuster.

Eddie Berganza & **Adam Schlagman** Editors
Robbin Brosterman Design Director – Books
Louis Prandi Art Director

DC COMICS
Diane Nelson President
Dan DiDio and **Jim Lee** Co-Publishers
Geoff Johns Chief Creative Officer
John Rood Executive Vice President, Sales, Marketing and Business Development
Patrick Caldon Executive Vice President, Finance and Administration
Amy Genkins Senior VP, Business and Legal Affairs
Steve Rotterdam Senior VP, Sales and Marketing
John Cunningham VP, Marketing
Terri Cunningham VP, Managing Editor
Alison Gill VP, Manufacturing
David Hyde VP, Publicity
Sue Pohja VP, Book Trade Sales
Alysse Soll VP, Advertising and Custom Publishing
Bob Wayne VP, Sales
Mark Chiarello Art Director

 EARTH ONE

Published by DC Comics, 1700 Broadway, New York, NY 10019. Copyright © 2010 by DC Comics. All rights reserved. All characters featured in this publication, the distinctive likenesses thereof and related elements are trademarks of DC Comics. Printed by RR Donnelley, Salem, VA, USA. 11/30/10 Second Printing. DC Comics, a Warner Bros. Entertainment Company.
HC ISBN: 978-1-4012-2468-4
SC ISBN: 978-1-4012-2469-1

DEDICATIONS

For as far back as I can remember, I would get a thrill of excitement every time I saw this symbol.

If you experienced the same thing, if you've ever worn that symbol on a T-shirt, doodled it on the back of a notebook, or had it tattooed on your arm... if you understand what that symbol means -- that all things are possible -- then this book is dedicated to you.

It is dedicated also to DC's Dan DiDio, who allowed this kid from New Jersey to finally realize the dream of a lifetime.

J. Michael Straczynski
Los Angeles, California
18 June 2010

Shane Davis would like to dedicate his artistic contribution to the memory of Shawn Davis. Shane would also like to give special thanks to Dan, John, Antonio, Michelle, Gabe, Mom and Dad.

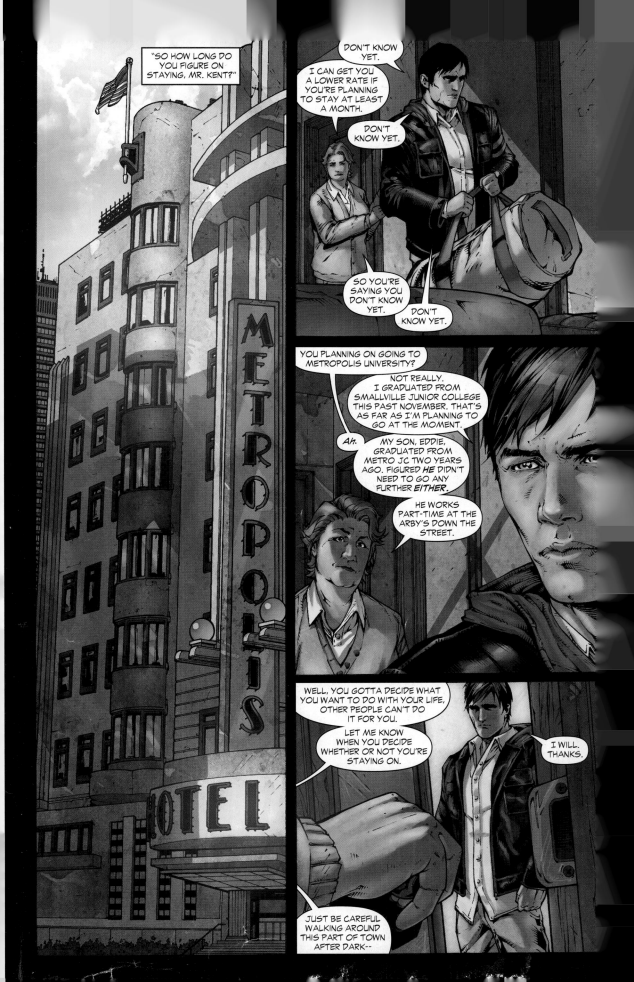

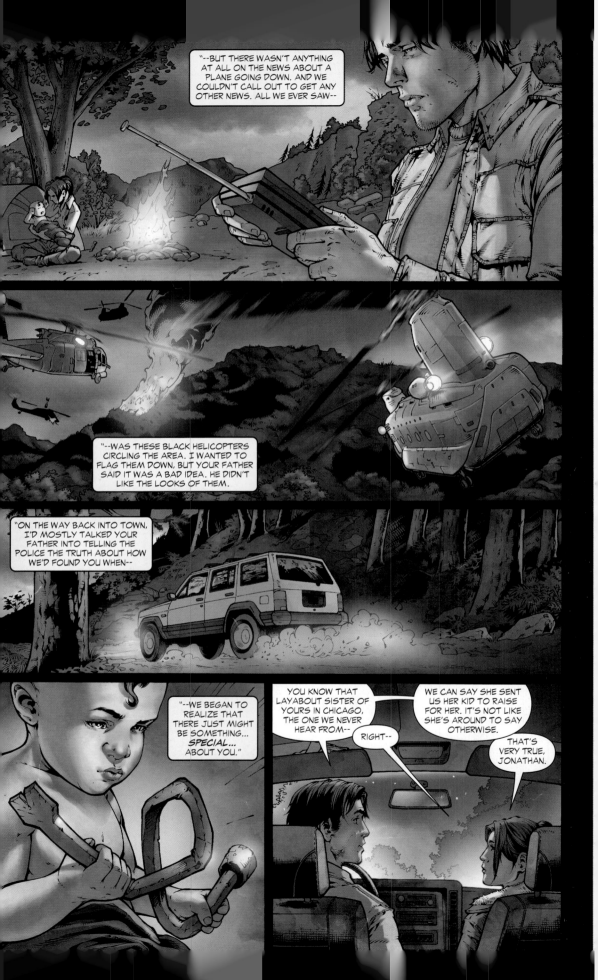

"--BUT THERE WASN'T ANYTHING AT ALL ON THE NEWS ABOUT A PLANE GOING DOWN. AND WE COULDN'T CALL OUT TO GET ANY OTHER NEWS. ALL WE EVER SAW--

"--WAS THESE BLACK HELICOPTERS CIRCLING THE AREA. I WANTED TO FLAG THEM DOWN, BUT YOUR FATHER SAID IT WAS A BAD IDEA. HE DIDN'T LIKE THE LOOKS OF THEM.

"ON THE WAY BACK INTO TOWN, I'D MOSTLY TALKED YOUR FATHER INTO TELLING THE POLICE THE TRUTH ABOUT HOW WE'D FOUND YOU WHEN--

"--WE BEGAN TO REALIZE THAT THERE JUST MIGHT BE SOMETHING... *SPECIAL*... ABOUT YOU."

YOU KNOW THAT LAYABOUT SISTER OF YOURS IN CHICAGO, THE ONE WE NEVER HEAR FROM--

RIGHT--

WE CAN SAY SHE SENT US HER KID TO RAISE FOR HER. IT'S NOT LIKE SHE'S AROUND TO SAY OTHERWISE.

THAT'S VERY TRUE, JONATHAN.

CLEARED TO ENTER CLEAN ROOM.

RETINAL SCAN CONFIRMED. DR. SANDRA LEE, MAJOR.

IS THERE *EVER* GOING TO BE A DAY WHEN I DON'T LOOK DOWN TO SEE YOU IN HERE, SANDRA? YOU EVER PLANNING TO TAKE A *SINGLE* DAY OFF TO ACTUALLY *ENJOY* YOURSELF?

IT TOOK SIXTY YEARS TO TRANSLATE THE ROSETTA STONE, DISCOVERED BY NAPOLEON'S FORCES IN 1798.

THE DEAD SEA SCROLLS, DISCOVERED IN 1947, ARE *STILL* BEING TRANSLATED.

WHEN YOU THINK ABOUT THE VALUE-- AND THE DANGER--OF WHAT THIS MAY REPRESENT FOR HUMANITY, A LITTLE OVER TWENTY YEARS IS NOTHING BY COMPARISON.

I'LL PARTY WHEN WE'RE DONE.

STAY CLOSE! POINT OF ORIGIN IS THE THIRD FLOOR!

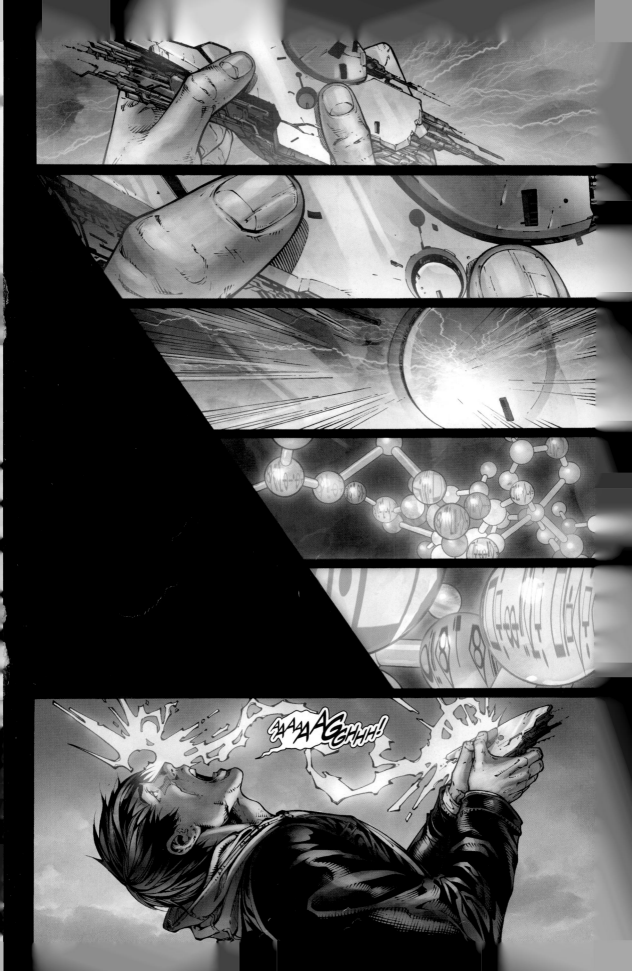

SAAAAAGHHH!

WHOMM

UNABLE TO PROCESS FULL DOWNLOAD WITHOUT ACCESS TO PRIMARY SYSTEMS.

ATTEMPTING TO ASCERTAIN LOCATION OF PRIMARY SYSTEMS.

ENGAGING PARTIAL SECONDARY SYSTEMS AS BACKUP.

TRANSMISSION TO COMMENCE IN THIRTY-POINT-SEVEN CHRONOMIKES.

"WHAT'S IT *DOING?*"

--SCRAMBLE ALL SQUADRONS, WEAPONS HOT, THIS IS NOT A DRILL, REPEAT, THIS IS NOT A DRILL--

TRACK AND TARGET BUT DO NOT FIRE UNLESS FIRED UPON. CENTCOMM IS IN THE PROCESS OF DETERMINING THEIR INTENT AND--

SSHRAACK

LOOKS LIKE WE'VE GAUGED THEIR INTENT.

ALL FIGHTERS, FORM UP AND ENGAGE! FIRE AT WILL!

"ROME.

"HONG KONG.

"LONDON.

"AND HERE AT HOME IN METROPOLIS, UNDER ATTACK BY THE LARGEST OF THE ATTACK SHIPS...WHICH WE BELIEVE IS THE COMMAND VESSEL."

COMMENCING DOWNLOAD.

HE WILL BE ALONE.

HE WILL BE *LIKE* THEM, BUT HE WILL NOT *BE* ONE OF THEM.

HE WILL BE *AMONG* THEM, BUT HE WILL NOT BE *OF* THEM.

I KNOW, LARA.

BUT HE WILL BE STRONG.

HE WILL BE NEARLY INDESTRUCTIBLE.

AND MOST IMPORTANT OF ALL, WHEN WE ARE LONG DEAD, HE WILL BE *ALIVE.*

"OR THAT THEIR TARGET, IF HE *IS* STILL ALIVE, DECIDES HE'S WILLING TO STEP OUT OF THE SHADOWS AND LET HIMSELF BE KILLED."

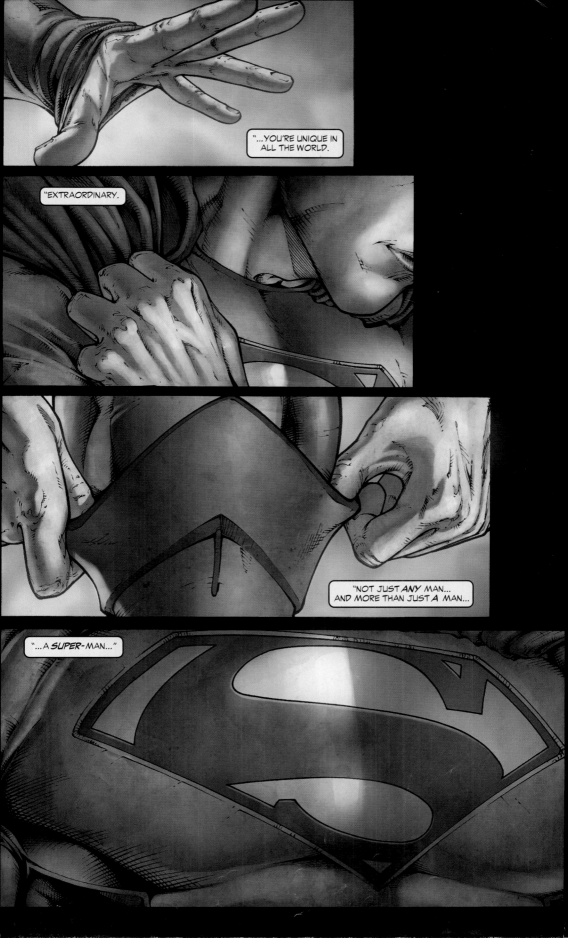

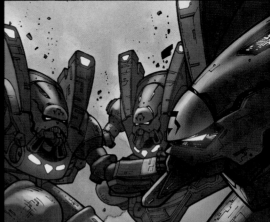

"TARGET ACQUIRED, ADVANCE FORCES ENGAGED."

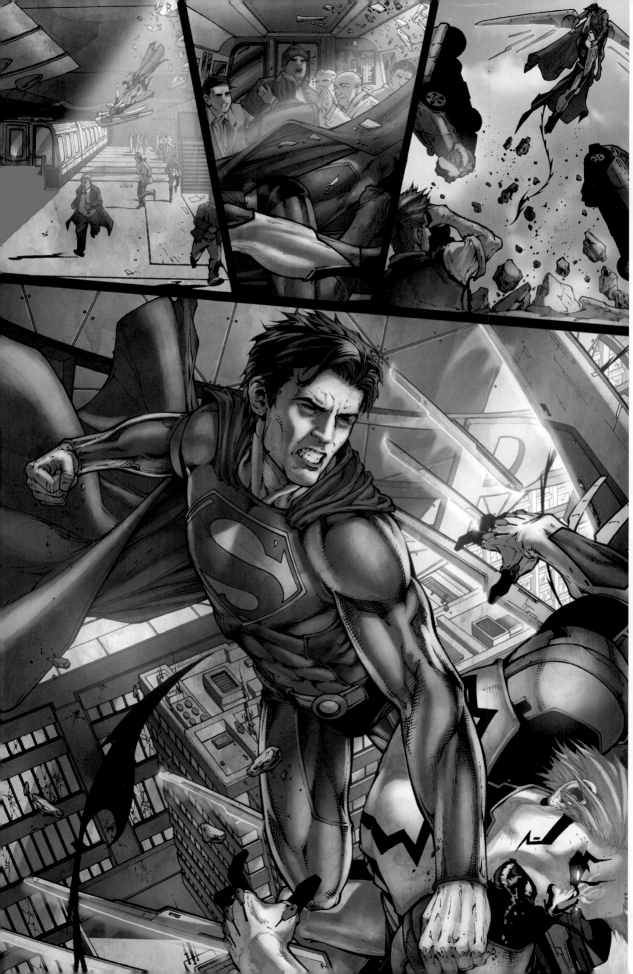

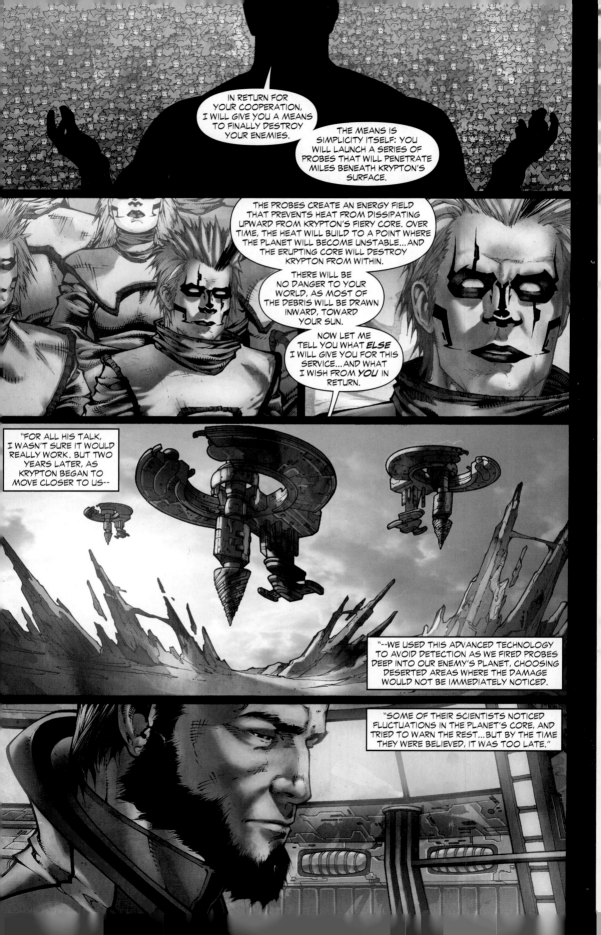

IN RETURN FOR YOUR COOPERATION, I WILL GIVE YOU A MEANS TO FINALLY DESTROY YOUR ENEMIES.

THE MEANS IS SIMPLICITY ITSELF: YOU WILL LAUNCH A SERIES OF PROBES THAT WILL PENETRATE MILES BENEATH KRYPTON'S SURFACE.

THE PROBES CREATE AN ENERGY FIELD THAT PREVENTS HEAT FROM DISSIPATING UPWARD FROM KRYPTON'S FIERY CORE. OVER TIME, THE HEAT WILL BUILD TO A POINT WHERE THE PLANET WILL BECOME UNSTABLE...AND THE ERUPTING CORE WILL DESTROY KRYPTON FROM WITHIN.

THERE WILL BE NO DANGER TO YOUR WORLD, AS MOST OF THE DEBRIS WILL BE DRAWN INWARD, TOWARD YOUR SUN.

NOW LET ME TELL YOU WHAT *ELSE* I WILL GIVE YOU FOR THIS SERVICE...AND WHAT I WISH FROM *YOU* IN RETURN.

"FOR ALL HIS TALK, I WASN'T SURE IT WOULD REALLY WORK. BUT TWO YEARS LATER, AS KRYPTON BEGAN TO MOVE CLOSER TO US--

"--WE USED THIS ADVANCED TECHNOLOGY TO AVOID DETECTION AS WE FIRED PROBES DEEP INTO OUR ENEMY'S PLANET, CHOOSING DESERTED AREAS WHERE THE DAMAGE WOULD NOT BE IMMEDIATELY NOTICED.

"SOME OF THEIR SCIENTISTS NOTICED FLUCTUATIONS IN THE PLANET'S CORE, AND TRIED TO WARN THE REST...BUT BY THE TIME THEY WERE BELIEVED, IT WAS TOO LATE."

"AND ON
THAT DAY..."

"UNDER THE TERMS OF OUR AGREEMENT,
NOT EVEN *ONE* OF KRYPTON'S CHILDREN
COULD BE ALLOWED TO SURVIVE. WE DID
NOT KNOW UNTIL MUCH LATER THAT ONE
OF THEIR SCIENTISTS WAS ABLE TO SEND
OUT A SHIP CONTAINING HIS PROGENY.

"WE SEARCHED FOR THAT SHIP
AND ITS PASSENGER ON EVERY
INHABITED WORLD THAT MIGHT
HAVE LAIN IN ITS PATH...A SEARCH
THAT HAS FINALLY LED US--"

RUSSIA.

EGYPT.

FRANCE.

TIBET.

AFRICA.

UNITED STATES.

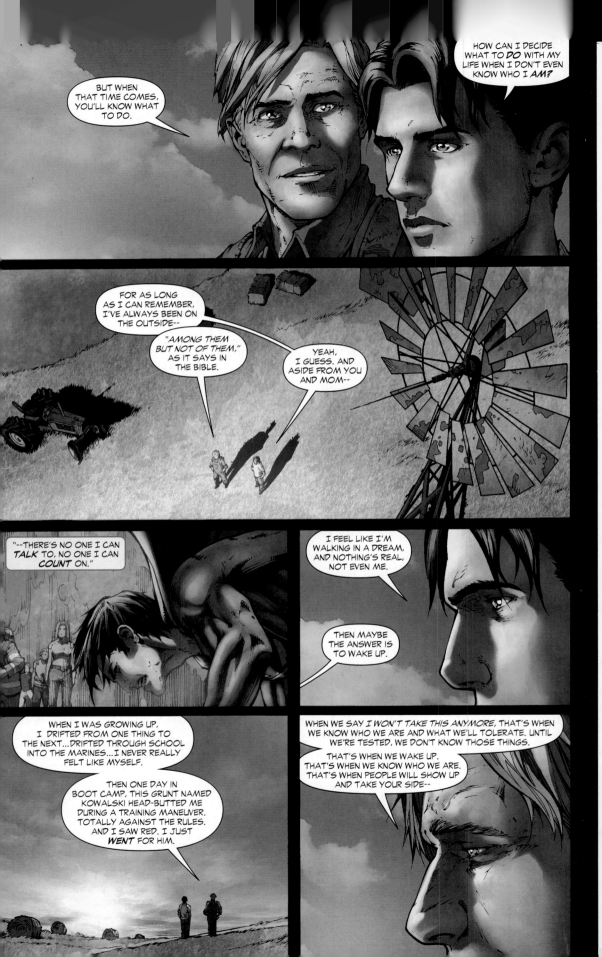

"--WHEN YOU DECIDE WHAT IT IS YOU *STAND* FOR, WHEN STANDING IS THE *HARDEST*."

HOLD ONTO THIS.

WHAT'RE YOU--

I DON'T WANT IT TO GET DAMAGED.

GGAAGGHHH!

CAN'T... MAKE IT... CAN'T...

COULDN'T MOVE...IT'S HELL IN THERE, FELT LIKE I WAS BEING CRUSHED--

"EVEN MY COMMAND SHIP HAS BEEN MADE OF METAL FROM MY HOME WORLD, WHICH UNDER THIS SUN IS NEARLY AS IMPERVIOUS AS KRYPTONIAN METAL."

PRIMARY SYSTEMS SYNCHRONIZATION AND RECONSTRUCTION COMPLETE.

PROCEEDING TO RENDEZVOUS WITH SUBJECT.

IT'S FINISHED...TOTALLY REBUILT.

I DON'T UNDERSTAND...WHY WOULD IT WAIT UNTIL *NOW* TO DO THIS?

MUST'VE BEEN SOME INTERNAL PROGRAMMING CREATED BY WHOEVER BUILT THIS, A SET OF INSTRUCTIONS THAT WOULD BE TRIGGERED BY SOME EXTERNAL CIRCUMSTANCE OR THREAT--

INITIATING ENGINE RESTART.

FIRE.

I *KNOW* THIS... I'VE BEEN *IN* THIS BEFORE.

KRYPTONIAN METAL...

HE SAID *NEARLY* AS IMPERVIOUS AS KRYPTONIAN METAL.

"YOU'VE BEEN HIDING YOUR WHOLE LIFE, CLARK. BUT IF YOU DO ANYTHING OTHER THAN WHAT I THINK YOU WERE *MEANT* TO DO, YOU'LL *STILL* BE HIDING, BECAUSE YOU'LL NEVER BE ABLE TO SHOW PEOPLE WHO YOU *REALLY* ARE, AND WHAT YOU CAN DO.

"LIFE WAS MEANT TO BE LIVED FULL MEASURE, FLAT OUT, PEDAL TO THE METAL. DON'T LIVE THE REST OF YOUR LIFE LIKE A PORSCHE THAT NEVER LEAVES THE GARAGE BECAUSE SOMEBODY'S AFRAID TO SCRATCH IT.

"*LIVE*, CLARK. FOLLOW YOUR PASSION. SHOW THE WHOLE *WORLD* WHAT YOU CAN DO.

"FLY, CLARK...

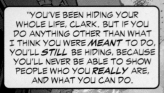

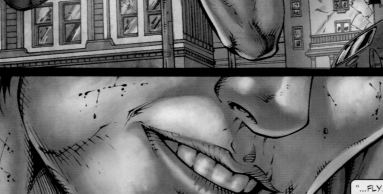

"...FLY..."

"...THE DAMAGE IS ESTIMATED TO BE IN THE BILLIONS WORLDWIDE."

MEANWHILE, OUR SATELLITES HAVE CONFIRMED THAT THE MAN IN BLUE HAS DESTROYED ALL OF THE DRILL UNITS.

GUESS HE DIDN'T WANT TO LEAVE THEM HANGING AROUND FOR SOMEBODY TO ACTIVATE THEM.

MY THOUGHT PRECISELY.

WHICH TELLS ME THAT HE'S WORRIED THAT WHOEVER SENT THIS FLEET AGAINST US MIGHT SEND ANOTHER ONE. OR AT LEAST, THAT'S THE WAY HE WANTS IT TO LOOK.

WHICH RAISES SEVERAL QUESTIONS.

IS IT POSSIBLE THIS ENTIRE THING WAS A SETUP, A FEINT TO GET US TO ACCEPT HIM AS OUR BENEFACTOR?

HE SEEMS TO HAVE SAVED EARTH. BUT DOES HIS CONTINUED PRESENCE CONTINUE TO ENDANGER US?

ULTIMATELY: WHO IS HE, AND WHAT DOES HE WANT?

YOU REMAIN CONFIDENT THAT HE CAME IN THE SHIP YOU'VE BEEN EXAMINING?

I AM, SIR. HIS AGE SEEMS TO CORRESPOND TO THE TIME SINCE WE DISCOVERED THE SHIP, AND IT WENT TO HIM LIKE A HUNTING DOG THAT JUST HEARD A WHISTLE.

THEN I'M PUTTING YOU IN CHARGE OF FINDING OUT AS MUCH AS CAN BE LEARNED ABOUT HIM.

YOU'LL HAVE EVERY AVAILABLE RESOURCE.

"BUT MAKE NO MISTAKE: I WANT HIM FOUND."

"THE MASK...

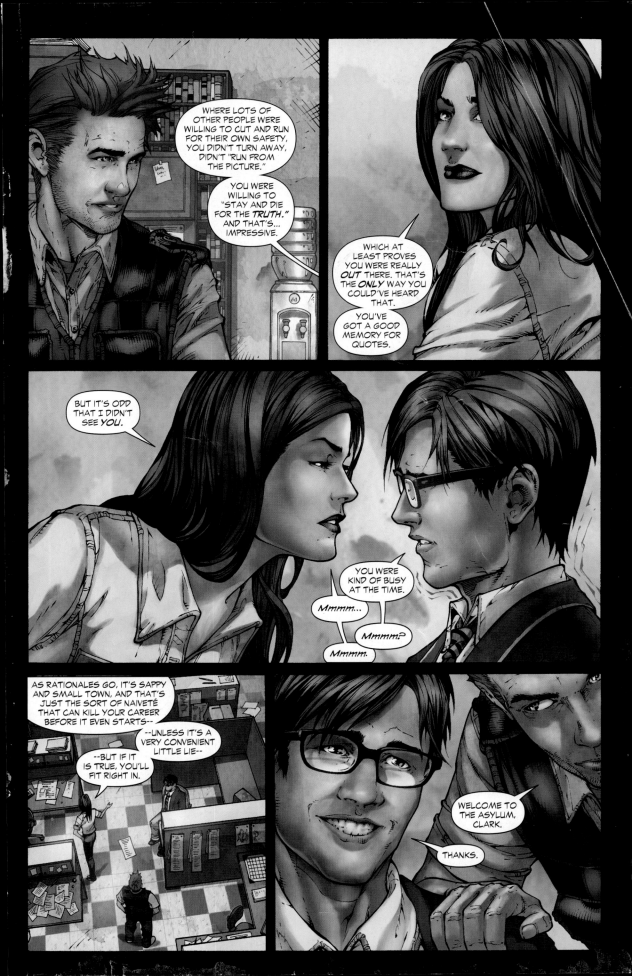

-- WHERE THAT GRAND DAME OF METROPOLIS JOURNALISM, THE *DAILY PLANET*, STUNNED THE NATION WITH ITS IN-DEPTH COVERAGE OF THE CRISIS, INCLUDING THE FIRST CLOSE-UP PHOTOS OF, AND AN INTERVIEW WITH, THE INDIVIDUAL NOW KNOWN AS SUPERMAN.

DAILY PLANET
"S" IS FOR...

WHAT DO YOU *MEAN* IT'S ALREADY OUT OF COPIES?

I TOLD MY GIRLFRIEND I'D GET TWO COPIES.

WHEN DOES THE NEXT EDITION COME OUT?

I THINK I SAW A NEWSSTAND AROUND THE CORNER.

SOLD OUT

WE HOPE TO HAVE SOME OF THOSE IMAGES AVAILABLE FOR YOU SHORTLY, ONCE WE OVERCOME CERTAIN... *TECHNICAL* DIFFICULTIES...

THE METROPOLIS TIMES WANTS PERMISSION TO USE SOME OF OUR PICTURES--

NO.

CNN...MSNBC... ABC...

NO.

THE *METRO-NEWS-DAILY*--

--CAN KISS MY--

AS FOR THE GENERAL PUBLIC, THE REACTIONS TO THE EVENTS OF THE LAST TWENTY-FOUR HOURS ARE DECIDEDLY MIXED.

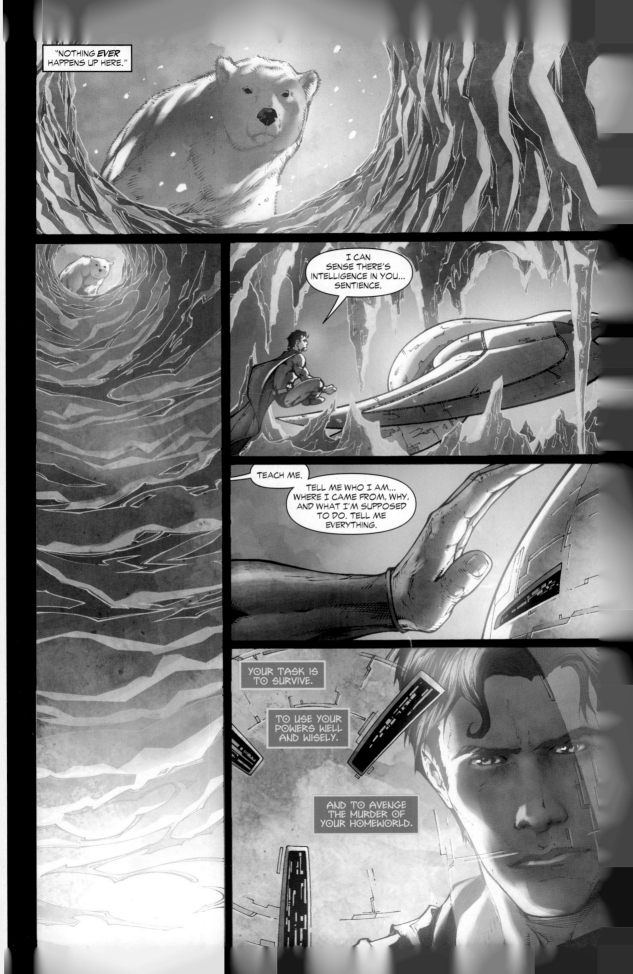

The End.

"S" IS FOR...

(DAILY PLANET photo by James Olsen)

...SUPERMAN. At least that's how he identified himself when he sat down for this exclusive interview with the *Daily Planet,* conducted in the aftermath of the recent crisis.

| By Clark Kent |
| Daily Planet |
| Staff Reporter |

Apparently in his twenties, he could be taken for a grad student on his way to Palm Beach for Spring Break except for the blue-and-red uniform, and the fact that he ent͟e͟r͟e͟d the room throu͟g͟h ͟ ͟ ͟ window...and it's ͟a͟ ten st͟

" O b v i o u s l y Superman isn't your real name," I say.

He smiles. "My father came up with it."

"Aren't you a bit nervous about how that name will be taken? I mean, isn't it a bit presumptuous?"

"I don't know, we'll have to see," he says. "I guess the important part is that there may be something super at the start of that name, but by the time you get to the end, it's still just a man."

He declines a polite request for his real name and the part of the country where he grew up, but from his tone of voice and vernacular, one could come to the conclusion that he was raised along the Eastern Seaboard. But as points of origin go, that's the least interesting one.

"If we can't know where you came from most recently, I suppose the next obvious question is, where were you born?"

"A distant world called Krypton. But understand: I came here as an infant, so I didn't know even that much of my history until recently. I knew I wasn't from around here, but beyond that… nothing."

"Have you had these powers your whole life?"

"Pretty much, yes. I remember the first time I flew, I was looking up at a bird flying overhead, and thinking how amazing that must be. Then I noticed that I was right next to it. For a second I thought it had come down to where I was, then I looked down and discovered that I was about fifty feet off the ground. Scared the heck out of me."

"So why the bright red-and-blue uniform?"

"The fabric, in the form of blankets, is all that came with me from Krypton. They can't be burned, torn, cut…or dyed, unfortunately. They're the only things I can wear without having them ripped off by wind or something else."

(DAILY PLANET photo by James Olsen)

"Too bad they didn't send along some blankets made of gray twill, maybe a nice charcoal."

He laughs in the fashion of someone who doesn't seem to do it a great deal. "See? That's what I'm talking about. I'm just lucky I didn't arrive surrounded by plaid blankets, or polka dot. That would be really hard to explain on a first date."

"So you're seeing someone?"

He shrugs. Smiles. "I have my eye on someone."

"So why did you wait so long before revealing yourself?"

"Wasn't any reason to do so earlier. What I can do wasn't needed before then." He hesitates for a moment, trying to find the right words. "Lincoln said that the proper role of government was to do that which individual people couldn't do for themselves. He added, 'you cannot help men permanently by doing for them what they could and should do for themselves.'"

"Sounds like you are advocating trickle-down heroics."

"Not at all. I'm just saying that until that ship showed up over Metropolis, everything

that came along in human history to that point could be handled by average men and women who could rise to the occasion. But no amount of rising was going to stop this."

"Like when the Balrog appears, and Gandalf says, 'swords are of no use here.'"

"Right, it's—"

"'This is beyond any of you.'"

I realize that I've revealed myself for the geek that I am, but he's polite enough not to comment on it. "Exactly. If I can help by doing things that the average person can't do for him- or herself, then that's what I want to do."

"So you're not planning on taking over the Earth."

He laughs. "No. I mean, what would I do with it? Where would I put it? Where do you park something like that?"

"Here's the thing," he says, his tone serious again. "I was raised in this country. I believe in this country. Does it have its flaws? Yes. Does it have its moments of greatness? Yes. Bottom line is, it's my home, and I'll always carry those values around with me. But if I do what I can do just for the U.S., it's going to destabilize

See SUPERMAN page 4

the whole world. It could even lead to war.

"So I'm here to do what I can, where I can, whether that's in the U.S. or elsewhere. But I can never get involved with politics or policy. There's nothing political about a tsunami, or an earthquake, or a tornado…nothing political about a gunman holding innocent hostages at a bank, or an out-of-control truck barreling down a crowded street. So those are the sorts of things I want to get involved with, where I can make a difference without becoming an instrument of policy."

"A lot of people are going to be unhappy to hear that. I think the Pentagon was already beginning to dream about your walking into China or Afghanistan and taking tanks apart, overthrowing governments and destroying whole fleets."

"And I understand that," he says. "But if I start down that road, then I can't serve humanity as a whole, which is what I feel I'm here to do. If I become an extension of any government or administration, then I lose the rest of the world, and there may be times when we'll need the rest of the world on board in the event of another planetary crisis."

He pauses for a moment, "I saw this documentary a few years ago about the British police force," he says, speaking slowly and deliberately, making his point. "They interviewed a London bobby who said—and I'm not taking sides, I'm just repeating what he said—that American police are there to enforce the peace, while the British police are there to create the peace.

"I like to think that's why I'm here: to help create the peace by doing what's right for people without trying to change them. Maybe that sounds naive, or superficial, but it's the truth."

DAILY PLANET photo by Jan Olser

- **WALL STREET REACTS TO RAMPAGE**
Aftereffects Felt in Markets Worldwide.
Dollar, Euro, Yen take hit.
In *FINANCE*

- **MONARCHS AND METEORS GAMES POSTPONED**
Monarchs to play day/nite doubleheader Saturday; Meteors game TBD.
In *SPORTS*

He looks out the window. It's getting dark. "I should head out, there's still a lot of work to be done clearing the streets and digging people out from under the mess."

"One last question, then. A hard one. There are going to be a lot of people who say this entire incident was your fault. After all, they did come here looking for you. What do you say to the families of the civilians, pilots and other military and police forces who died fighting the intruders?"

— *See SUPERMAN page 5*

SUPERMAN

Continued from page 4

He looks at his hands. Hands that could tear down a mountain without even trying. But right now, they seem lost. "I don't know," he says at last. "I wish I had a good answer. I wish I knew the words that would comfort those who have lost loved ones, or were hurt. Nothing can ever make those wounds go away, ever fill those empty spaces. Which proves that there are some things impossible even for a Superman.

"But I will say this. I didn't know they were out there, didn't know they were after me, didn't know any of this until the day they showed up. I found out about it the same time everybody else did. So while what happened may not technically be my fault, it is my responsibility, and I will live with that knowledge every day for the rest of my life. Every morning, when I open my eyes, I'll know that I'm here, and that this world is here, in part because of the sacrifices made by those people on this day. And I will dedicate every breath I take, every action I take, to their memory. I don't know if that scale can ever be truly balanced, but I do know that I'm willing to give my life trying to measure up to their sacrifice.

"See, that's the remarkable thing, and the irony," he says, rising and moving toward the window. "As someone who can look at humanity from the outside, I see your amazing strengths, your stubborn nobility, your greatness and your kindness and your generosity and your willingness to aspire, to sacrifice, to struggle over the mountaintop no matter how big the boulders are coming your way. I am blinded by the light that burns inside every one of you.

"In that light, one truth emerges: if the word 'super' is to be applied to anyone, it should be applied to all of you, to all of mankind. Against that power, against that truth… I'm just a man."

And then he was gone.

(DAILY PLANET photo by James Olsen)

EDITORIAL

Under a Broken Sky

DAILY PLANET PERSPECTIVE

By Lois Lane
Daily Planet Staff Reporter

METROPOLIS — As a young girl, I was a history nut. In particular I loved reading about Edward R. Murrow, Walter Cronkite and other reporters who chronicled the bombing of London from the inside during the Second World War. I wondered what it would be like to cover a city under seige, and even as a working reporter imagined that the only way I could find out would be to travel somewhere else, to file stories from places like Lebanon or Beirut or Iraq, since after all, those things never happened inside the United States. It was always over there, somewhere.

Yesterday, all that changed.

Yesterday, the sky was broken open, and from that wound something profound and dangerous entered the life of this city, this country, and this world. Yesterday, far-flung, distant peoples in every corner of the globe were united in the possibility of annhilation. Yesterday, we stood at the edge of the abyss.

Yesterday, today seemed impossible. But today has come, and we still stand, in large part due to the arrival of one man, who stood with us against impossible odds.

And because of this man, we now have a tomorrow we did not expect. He is, truly, the man of tomorrow.

Earth One Sketch Book

Here and on the preceding pages are Shane Davis's initial design work for Clark Kent, the Man of Steel and his foes.

This was no small undertaking; the artist had to make everything feel fresh and new, while maintaining the iconic look of the character.

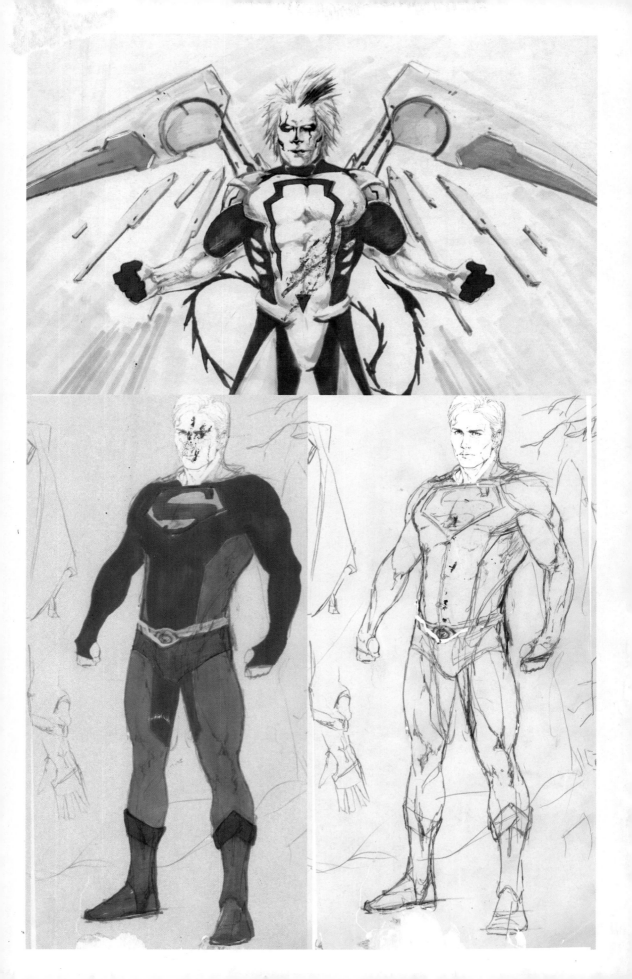

J. MICHAEL STRACZYNSKI is an award-winning writer for film, television and comics. A former journalist for the Los Angeles Times and TIME Inc., he has worked on such series as *The Twilight Zone* and *Murder She Wrote*, and created *Jeremiah, Crusade* and *Babylon 5*, for which he may be best known. He penned the screenplay for Clint Eastwood's *Changeling*, for which he received a British Academy Award nomination, and *Ninja Assassin* for the Wachowskis. His work has earned him two Hugo Awards, as well as the Saturn, the Eisner, the Inkpot and the Ray Bradbury Award, among many others. His comics work includes *Rising Stars* and *Midnight Nation* for Top Cow/Image, *The Amazing Spider-Man*, *Supreme Power*, and *Thor* for Marvel, and he now writes both SUPERMAN and WONDER WOMAN for DC Comics.

SHANE DAVIS is an award-winning American comic book artist. Shane's pencils have appeared in JUSTICE LEAGUE OF AMERICA: THE LIGHTNING SAGA, MYSTERY IN SPACE and SUPERMAN/BATMAN: THE SEARCH FOR KRYPTONITE.

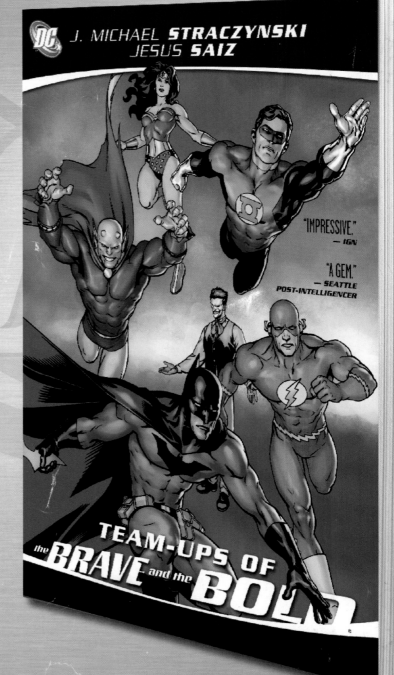